WHERE DOES

the food in your fridge come from?

By Ronne Randall

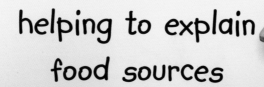

helping to explain
food sources

WHERE DOES

the food in your fridge come from?

MEDIA

Copyright © ticktock Entertainment Ltd 2003

First published in Great Britain in 2003 by ticktock Media Ltd.,

Unit 2, Orchard Business Centre, North Farm Road, Tunbridge Wells, Kent, TN2 3XF

We would like to thank: Lorna Cowan, Rod Knutton and Elizabeth Wiggans.

ISBN 1 86007 386 7 pbk

ISBN 1 86007 392 1 hbk

Printed in Egypt

A CIP catalogue record for this book is available
from the British Library.

CONTENTS

Any words appearing in the text
in bold, **like this**, are explained
in the Glossary.

Have you ever wondered where the food you eat comes from?

4

The supermarket   **The baker**   **The farm**

Maybe you buy all your food at the supermarket.
Maybe you get some from the baker, or the greengrocer,
or even from the farm.

But have you ever wondered how the food gets there?

How is it made? What is it made from?

5

What are French fries made from?

French fries are made from potatoes. Potatoes grow in fields on farms.

But you can grow potatoes in your garden too.

When potatoes are quite old they start to sprout.

Sprouting potatoes

If you **plant** these potatoes in the ground each one will grow into more potatoes!

The potato sprouts grow into **shoots** underground.

The shoots appear through the soil and grow into potato plants with flowers.

The potatoes are ready to be dug up when the flowers turn yellow and die.

Can you think of another popular snack food that is made from potatoes?

(answer on page 23)

The potatoes need to be washed and the skins peeled off.

Then they can be cut into fries, and deep fried in hot oil.

Enjoy your French fries!

What goes with French fries and is made from tomatoes?

a) Mustard

b) Mayonnaise

c) Ketchup

(You will find the answer on the next page.)

What food is made from tomatoes?

Ketchup is made from tomatoes. The tomatoes grow on plants.

The plants grow in rows, on farms. Before they are **ripe** the tomatoes are green.

Is a tomato a vegetable or a fruit?

(answer on page 23)

When the tomatoes are red they are ready to be picked. A machine collects them and puts them into big bins.

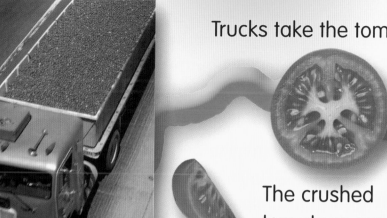

Trucks take the tomatoes to the ketchup factory.

At the factory, the tomatoes are crushed in a vat.

The crushed tomatoes are mixed with salt, sugar, spices and vinegar.

A vat

The mixture is cooked, cooled and put into bottles.

Do you like ketchup on your burgers and fries?

What is bread made from?

a) Wheat

b) Beans

c) Potatoes

What is bread made from?

Bread is made from wheat. Farmers **plant** wheat in fields.

As the wheat gets bigger an **ear** grows at the top. This is where the wheat **grains** are.

Wheat ear

Do you know what straw is used for?

(answer on page 23)

At **harvest** time a **combine harvester** cuts down the wheat. The grains are separated.

Wheat grains

The rest of the plant is left in the field to dry into straw

10

The farmer sells the grain to the flour mill.

At the mill, the grains are crushed to make flour. The flour is sold to bakeries and shops.

Grain

At the bakery, water, sugar and yeast are added to make **dough**.

Flour

The dough is **kneaded** and baked in the oven...

...and comes out as bread!

Where do eggs come from?

a) Plants

b) Birds

c) From under the ground

11

Where do eggs come from?

Eggs come from hens.
Hens are female chickens.

Hens live on **poultry** farms,
mostly in cages, in hen
houses. **Free-range**
hens live outside.

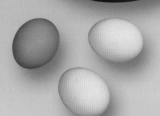

Each hen lays an egg
almost every day.

Grain

Hens eat lots of grain –
about 36 kilos a year!

The eggs are collected underneath the cages. Rollers gently send the eggs to the packing area where they are packed on plastic trays.

Next the eggs are sent to a **grading station**. They are washed and **candled**, to make sure they are not cracked or damaged.

Then the eggs are sorted by size and put in cartons.

What other birds lay eggs that people eat?

(answer on page 23)

The next stop is the shop – and then your breakfast table!

Which of these foods comes from cows?

a) Cheese and butter

b) Ice cream

c) Yogurt

Which foods come from cows?

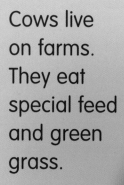

Butter, ice cream, yogurt and cheese are all made from milk..

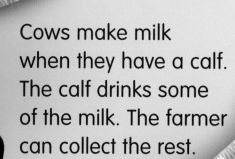

...and milk comes from cows!

Cows live on farms. They eat special feed and green grass.

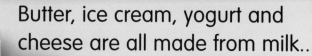

Cows make milk when they have a calf. The calf drinks some of the milk. The farmer can collect the rest.

Udder

A milking machine is attached to the cow's **udder**. Milk comes out of the udder and is pumped into a storage tank.

Tank trucks take the milk to a **dairy**.

What other animals make milk that you can drink?

(answer on page 23)

Some milk goes to factories to make cheese, yogurt, butter and ice cream.

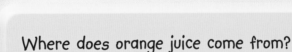

The milk is **pasteurized** to kill any germs, and some of the cream is removed. The milk is poured into cartons and bottles.

Then it is delivered to the supermarket or to your doorstep!

Where does orange juice come from?

a) An animal
b) A fruit tree
c) Under the ground

Where does orange juice come from?

Orange juice comes
from oranges.

Oranges are **fruits**,
and they grow on
trees, in orange **groves**.

The trees grow in places
like Brazil, Spain and in
Florida, in the USA.
These places are
warm and sunny
almost all year round.

When the oranges are **ripe** they are
picked by hand and put into big bins.

A truck takes the oranges to a factory.

The oranges are put on a **conveyor belt**. They are washed, then sent to the **extractors**, which squeeze out the juice.

The juice is **pasteurized** to kill germs.

Can you think of other fruits that are made into juice?

(answer on page 23)

It is poured into cartons and bottles. Drink up!

What kind of a plant is rice?

a) A kind of grass

b) A kind of fruit tree

c) A kind of cactus

What kind of a plant is rice?

Rice is actually a kind of grass. It is a **cereal** plant.

Rice is grown in a field called a paddy. The paddy is flooded with water, about 5 to 10 cm deep.

The rice needs to stay covered with water while it grows.

When the rice is ready to **harvest** it is picked by hand or by a machine.

Can you think of another cereal plant?

(answer on page 23)

The rice is dried and taken to a mill.

At the mill, the rice **kernels** are separated from the **husks**.

Broken rice kernels are crushed to make rice flour. The husks are used to make animal feed.

The whole rice kernels are sent to factories. The rice is packed into sacks and boxes, ready to be cooked!

What is chocolate made from?

a) Bugs
b) Birds
c) Beans

What is chocolate made from?

Chocolate is made from cocoa beans. Cocoa beans are the **seeds** of the cacao tree fruit.

Cacao tree fruit

The fruits are picked, and the beans are left to dry in the Sun.

Cacao trees grow in warm, **tropical** countries like Brazil and Indonesia.

The dried cocoa beans go to the chocolate maker to be **roasted** and crushed into a **liquid**.

Cocoa beans

Some of the liquid is dried to make cocoa powder.

Chocolate paste

Sugar and milk are added to the liquid, and it is blended into a paste.

The paste is heated and allowed to cool slowly. Nuts or fruit can be added now.

Can you think what cocoa powder is used for?

(answer on page 23)

The paste is poured into **moulds**. As it gets cooler it goes hard.

Now the bars of chocolate are ready for wrapping – then unwrapping and eating!

Glossary

Candled When an egg is held up against a bright light so its insides can be seen, to make sure it is in good condition.

Cereal A grass whose grains are used for food.

Combine harvester A machine that cuts down cereal plants, cleans them and separates the grains (seeds) from the straw.

Conveyor belt A machine in a factory that has a long, wide belt that moves things along without stopping.

Dairy A place where milk is prepared before it is sold.

Dough A mixture of flour and water. It is baked to make bread.

Ear The part of a cereal plant that holds the seeds.

Extractors Machines that remove or separate parts of something. In an orange juice factory, extractors squeeze the juice out of the fruit.

Free-range Farm animals that are free to move around a yard or field, and look for food, instead of being kept in cages.

Fruits Foods like apples, oranges and pears that grow on plants, vines or trees.

They have seeds inside them.

Grading station A place where eggs are sent to be checked and measured, before being sorted into cartons and sent to shops.

Grains The seeds of a cereal plant.

Groves Groups of fruit trees planted together.

Harvest To pick or gather crops or fruit that are ready to eat.

Husks The outer shells of seeds. They are usually taken off and thrown away.

Kernels The parts of seeds that

are inside the husks.

Kneaded To fold, press and stretch dough into shape before baking it.

Liquid Something that is runny. Water is a liquid.

Moulds Shaped containers that hold something runny while it hardens.

Pasteurized When milk or orange juice has been made very hot in order to kill germs.

Plant To put something in the soil so it can grow.

Poultry Birds like chickens, turkeys and ducks, which are raised for their eggs or meat.

Ripe When a fruit or vegetable is fully grown and ready to be picked for eating.

Roasted To cook something in an oven until it is dry and becomes dark in colour.

Seeds Small parts of a plant that can grow into a new plant.

Shoots The beginning of a new plant that comes from a seed.

Tropical A place where the weather is hot and sunny most of the time.

Udder The part of a cow where milk is made.

Could you answer all the questions? Here are the answers:

Page 7: Crisps are made from potatoes.

Page 8: Most people think tomatoes are vegetables, but they are fruits! Fruits have seeds inside them – most vegetables don't.

Page 10: Straw can be used as animal food and bedding, for weaving into baskets and for thatching roofs.

Page 13: Some people eat duck, goose and quail eggs.

Page 15: People drink goats' milk and sheeps' milk. They make cheese from the milk as well.

Page 17: We can get juice from almost any fruit, but some of the most popular fruit juices are orange, apple, grapefruit, grape and pineapple.

Page 19: Wheat, oats, barley, sweetcorn (maize) and rye are all cereal plants.

Page 21: Cocoa powder is used to make drinking chocolate and for making chocolate cake.

Index

t=top, b=bottom, c=centre, l=left, r=right, OFC=outside front cover, OBC=outside back cover

Alamy images: OFC, 1tl, 4bl, 5tc, 8br, 9tl, 11c, 12tr, 12bl, 13t, 15tl, 15cr, 16tl, 18br, 19t, 19cl, 20tr, 20bl. Corbis: 1cl, 1bl, 1tr, 1cr, 1br, 2tl, 2bl, 2tr, 2br, 3tl, 3bl, 3tr, 3br, 4tl, 4tc, 4tr, 5tl, 5tr, 5b, 6tl, 7tr, 7b, 8tr, 10tl, 10tr, 10bl, 10br, 11t, 11bl, 12tl, 12br, 13bl, 14, 16tr, 16bl, 17, 19cr, 20br, 21br. Science Photo Library: 9cr.

Every effort has been made to trace the copyright holders and we apologize in advance for any unintentional omissions. We would be pleased to insert the appropriate acknowledgements in any subsequent edition of this publication.